A SIMPLE AND SHORT GUIDE OF PYTHON FOR BEGINNERS

2

Contents

3

Forward

What does Python programming begin with?

Python constitutes a dynamic, byte code-compiled, and interpreted language. Variable, parameter, function, and method types are not declared in the source code. You sacrifice the source code's compile-time type verification but get short, flexible code as a result.

What is programming in Python?

High-level programming languages like Python are used in general-purpose software engineering. It processes the logic behind inputs from users, communicates with databases along with additional servers, etc. since it is a server side language, which means it operates on the server.

Along with other server-side languages include Java and C, Python has already been around since it was first created in the late 1980s by Guido Van Rossum. In order to make Python simpler to understand and write than various other programming languages, Van Rossum patterned it after the English language and removed superfluous syntax.

Python is a language that is open-source that has gained popularity in recent years as a result of its application in data science. In addition, a large number of tools and modules have been created specifically for machine learning, statistical data analysis, and artificial intelligence (AI) in Python.

History of python

Popular high-level, all-purpose programming language Python. It was first developed by Guido van Rossum, then by the Python Software Foundation. Thanks to its emphasis on code readability, programmers may convey ideas using its syntax and fewer lines of code.

It was going to be the late 1980s when history was written. Python development started at that point. Guido Van Rossum soon after began working on application-based projects in Netherlands-based Center for Wiskunde and Informatics (CWI), which in December 1989. He first started it as a hobby project since he was looking for something entertaining to do during the holidays. The ABC

Programming Language, which Python is credited for outperforming, included exception handling and interacted with the Amoeba Operating System. In the beginning of his career, he had helped to establish ABC. Although he had seen certain issues with ABC, he generally liked its features. The next action he took was really rather wise. He had included some of the beneficial elements and syntax of ABC. He totally addressed those issues and created a powerful scripting language that was faultless as a result of the feedback it received. He named it Python because he was a huge fan of the BBC television show "Monty Python's Flying Circus" and wanted a catchy, memorable, and somewhat intriguing name for his invention. Up until his resignation as leader on July 12th, 2018, he presided as the "Benevolent dictator for life" (BDFL). He used to work for Google for a time, but right now he works for Drop box.

Why at that time study Python?

1. Python is very flexible and has many applications.

Data Mining, Data Engineering, Machine Learning, AI, Web Development, the internet Frameworks, Embedded Systems, Illustration Programs, Gaming, Network Development, Development of Products, Rapid Development of Applications, Testing, Automation Scripting, and the list goes on are just a few of the most popular applications for Python.

Python is utilized as a simpler and more effectively written replacement to languages like C, R, and Java that carry out identical functionality. As a result, Python is increasingly used as the primary dialect for many applications.

Machine learning and data mining use Python.

R has always been the programming language of choice for data scientists. Python has grown in popularity for data science, particularly among workers without formal expertise in statistics or mathematical sciences. Python code is seen to be simpler to maintain and more scalable than R.

Many Python packages have been created in the last few years for machine learning and data analysis. This comprises pyspark, an API for interacting with Spark, a framework for quickly working with huge data sets, tensor flow, which is used to write machine learning algorithms, and jumpy and pandas, which enable users to comprehend and change data.

To install and execute Python on your computer, follow these instructions.

- Get Thonny IDE now.
- To set up Thonny on your PC, launch the installer.
- Navigate to File > New. Once saved, give the file a.py extension.
- Hello.py, example.py, etc., as examples.
- The file may have any name you like. Nevertheless, the filename should finish in.py.
- Create a file, add Python code, and save it.
- Next, choose Run > Run Current Script or just press F5 to launch it.

Install Python on its own

o   Here is a guide on how to install and run Python on your PC if you don't want to use Thonny.

o   Download Python's most recent release.

o   Run the installation file and adhere to the instructions to set up Python.

o   Check the installation procedure To environment variables, add Python. Python will then be added to the environment variables, allowing for execution from any location on the machine.

o   You may also choose the location of Python's installation.

What are Python's underlying principles?

The syntax of Python is straightforward and resembles that of English. Python's syntax sets it apart from plenty of other languages of programming by making it possible for programmers to build applications with less code. Python's translation system makes it possible for written code to run instantly.

Python foundations

With our beginner-friendly lessons, you may begin your Python career.

You'll discover key ideas for Python novices on this page that will assist you in getting started utilizing the language. These courses are intended to teach you the very essentials of Python.

What are variables in Python, with an example?

Data is stored in variables, which need memory space depending on the sort of value we give to them. It's easy to create variables in Python; simply put the variable name on the left side of the equal sign (=) and the value on the right, as seen below. What are Python's four different sorts of variables?

o   Python's Numeric Variable Styles.

o   Text Format.

o   (Python list, Python tuple,

o   or Python range) Sequence Type

o   Boolean. Set. Dictionary.

What does a Python data type mean?

Using Python's Data Types | 6 Common Python Data Types

- o Knowledge objects are categorized or classified using data kinds.
- o Numeric, String, List,
- o Tuple, Set, and Dictionary are the six common data types in Python.
- o In Python, how do you provide the data type?

Data Types in Functions: Specifying

The input parameters a and b, which indicate the integer type, are followed by the additional:. This implies that the function's parameters and b should be of the integer type. Additionally, take note of the -> int that follows the input parameters.

Which data types are there in Python?

The following list of built-in data types for Python will be covered in this tutorial: Integer, float, and complex numbers. str is a string. Sequence: range, tuple, and list.

What do Python operators do?

Python's operators and expressions - Real Python

Operators in Python are specialized symbols that indicate that a certain kind of calculation should be carried out. Operands are the values that an operator manipulates. Here's an illustration:

>>> >>> a = 10 >>> b = 20 >>> a + b

30. In this instance, the operands a and b are added together via the + operator.

What do Python's eight operators do?

.

- o Operators in Python
- o Operators in mathematics.
- o Operators for assignments.
- o Operators for comparison.
- o Operators of logic.
- o Operator identities.
- o Operators of memberships.
- o operators for bits

What does a Python statement variable do?

Variables in Python - The Real Python

In Python, a variable is a symbolic name that references or points to an object. After a variable has been assigned to an object, it may still be used to refer to that object. The information is still there on the item, however. For example, n = 300.

What are the three statements in Python?

Print messages, assignment assertions, conditions, and looping statements are the four subcategories of statements in Python. The use of print plus assignment statements is customary.

How are statements executed in Python?

Each of the statements is executed in ascending order, one at a time. Function declarations have no impact on the order in which a program executes, but you should be aware that statements in a function are not executed until the function is called. The execution process is interrupted by function calls.

What do Python functions do?

Previous following a piece of code is a section of code that only executes when called. You may provide parameters—data—to a function. As a result, a function may return data.

What are Python's four different sorts of functions?

- o Python Function Tutorial: Different Types of Python Functions (With...
- o Additionally, we will examine the many kinds of functions in Python, including built-in, recursive,
- o lambda, and user-defined functions,
- o Along with their syntax & examples.

What do Python's conditional statements do?

Examples of If Statements in Python: How to Use Conditional...

The basic building blocks of programming are conditional statements (if, else, and elif), which let you direct the course of your program in response to certain situations. They provide a means for your software to make choices and execute various pieces of code in response to those decisions.

Does Python support all four forms of conditional statements?

Conditional Statements in Python: Elif, If_else, and Nested Statement If Our program's execution is governed by many sorts of conditional statements, including if, if-else, elif, nested if, and nested if-else expressions.

What is a conditional statement example?

Example: A conditional statement is present. In the event of rain, we will not play. Let's say A: It's raining and B: We're not going to play. If A is true—that is, if it is raining—and B is false—that is, if we played—then A implies that B is untrue.

What does a Python loop do?
Looping is the process of repeatedly doing something up until a certain condition is fulfilled. As long as the condition is met, a for loop in Py is an expression of control flow that is used to continually execute a set of instructions.

How is the Python for loop written?
Python's Basic for Loop Syntax the iterate is represented by the letter i. It may be changed to anything you choose.

Any inerrable, including lists, tuples, strings, and dictionaries, is referred to as data.

The next thing you need to enter is a colon, followed by an indent. Tab may be used for this, or you can hit the spacebar four times.

What are Python's three different forms of loops?

It enables programmers to change the program's flow such that they may only repeat the code a limited number of times rather than repeating the same code again. For loops, while loops, and nested loops are the three main forms of loops available in Python.

- **Lists**

Are a collection of inerrable, changeable, and ordered data and are among the most frequently used data structures offered by Python. They could include redundant data.

- **Tuple**

Lists and multiples are comparable. Similar to lists, this collection includes iterable, sorted, and (may include) repeating data. Tuples, however, are immutable, unlike lists.

- **Set**

Set is a different kind of data structure that stores a collection of iterable, modifiable, and unordered data. But it merely has distinctive components.

Dictionary

Dictionary collections only hold key-value pairs, in contrast to all other collection types.

is a collection of unsorted data in Python version 3.7.

A new form of dictionary named "OrderedDict," which was comparable to Python's dictionary but different in that it was ordered (as the name implies), was introduced in Python v3.1.

Using Python 3.7, the most recent version, you can: Finally, dictionary is now an organized collection of key-value pairs in Python 3.7. Now that they have been put, the order is assured to be in that order.

What do instances, classes, and objects mean?

A particular kind of blueprint that you may use to create things is a class. An object, which is an instance of a class, is a tangible "thing" that you created using a certain class. The link between an object and its class is what the word "instance" refers to, even though the terms "object" and "instance" is equivalent.

In OOP, what do class and instance mean?

An item formed from a class is called an instance. The instance's present state is determined by the operations carried out on it, while the class specifies the instance's (behavior and information) structure.

Overview of Python Modules

In fact, Python has three alternative methods for defining modules:

Python itself may be used to create modules.

- A module, similar to the res (regular expression) module,
- May be built in C and loaded flexibly at runtime.
- Like the itertools module, a built-in module is innately present in the interpreter.

The import statement is used in each of the three scenarios to access a module's contents.

Here, Python modules will be primarily the subject of discussion. The wonderful thing about Python modules is that they are quite simple to create. All you have to do is create a file containing authentic Python code and give it a name ending in.py. I'm done now! No voodoo or specific syntax is required.

For instance, let's say you wrote the following code in a file named mod.py:

mod.py

If Comrade Napoleon says that, it must be true, so says s.

```
a = [100, 200, 300]
```

```
Defined in function foo(arg):
print(f'arg = 'arg')
```

```
pass for class Foo
```

Develop a Module

Simply place the desired code in a file with the.py file extension to build a module.

Example Purchase a Python server. Put this code in a file called mymodule.py and save it.

```
def salutation (name):
  print("Hello," name," "")
```

Apply a Module

Now, using the import line, we can utilize the module we just created:

Example

Call the welcome function and import the my module module:

bring up my module

mymodule.greeting("Jonathan")

How do I make a Python module package?

Simply place the desired code in a file with the.py file extension to build a module.

Example Purchase a Python server.

Call the welcome function and import the module.

This code should be saved in the file mymodule.py.

Access the person1 dictionary and import the module my module:

Python Input and Output

How to Get User Input in Python Occasionally, a programmer may wish to get user input during some point throughout the program. Python has the input() method to do this.

Syntax:

Where reminder is an optional line that is shown on the string while input is being accepted.

Example 2: Input from the user as an integer in Python # num = int(input("Enter a number: "))

= num + 1 + add

Produced by print(add)

Output:

Type a number here: 25 26
How to accept several Inputs in Python: The map() function in Python allows us to accept several inputs of the same data type at once.

A, B, and C are equal to map(int, "Enter the Numbers:").print(split())
"The Numbers are: ",end = "
write (a, b, c)
Output:

To enter, type 2 3 4
The digits are: 2, 3, and 4.

What does managing errors in Python mean?

Dictionary for Python. The try block allows you to check a block of code for errors. The unless block may be used to fix the error. You may still execute code by using the finally block, regardless of the results of the try- and except blocks.

How should Python errors be handled properly?

Better Python Error Handling: 7 Tips

- Explicit is preferable than implicit. The following clauses apply to Python's exceptions: Nesting is not preferred than flat.
- Make special exclusions.
- Keep your try/except block width small.

- Use them in practice.
- a lot of logging.
- (Remote settings) Utilize tools

Benefits of Python

- Generous Libraries
- Python comes with a sizable library that can be downloaded, and it has code for a variety of things, like regular expressions, databases, CGI, email, image processing, and more. It can also generate documentation, run unit tests, run web browsers, and thread code.

- Therefore, we don't need to manually write the whole code for it.

- Flexible
- Other languages may be added to Python. Some of your code may be written in C++ or C, for example.

- This is useful, particularly for projects.

- Embedded
- Python also has embed ability, which is complementary to extensibility. Python code may be inserted into the source code of another language, such as C++.

- This enables us to add scripting functionality to our other language code.

- Enhanced Productivity
- Programmers are more productive than they are with languages like Java and C++ because to the language's simplicity and large library.

- Additionally, you should write less and do more things.

- 5. IOT Possibilities
- Python believes that the Internet of Things has a bright future since it serves as the foundation for cutting-edge platforms like Raspberry Pi.

- This helps to link the language to the outside world.

- 6. Easy and Simple
- You may need to construct a class in Java to print "Hello World." But all you need with Python is a print statement.

- Additionally, it is quite simple to learn, comprehend, and code.

- 7. Accessible
- Reading Python is quite similar to reading English since it is not a very verbose language. This explains why learning, comprehending, and coding are so simple.

- Block definitions may be made without curly braces, and indentation is required. This improves the code's readability much further.

- 8. Object-orientation
- Both the procedural and object-oriented programming paradigms are supported by this language.

- Classes and objects allow us to simulate the actual world, while functions assist us with code reuse.

Drawback. Python

- Python's pace is slower than that of Java or C, which is a drawback. Python is an interpreter, dynamically typed language. Since the language is interpreted during code execution, each line of the code must be explicitly arranged. The execution procedure is slowed down by this since it takes a lot of time. Python's dynamic structure additionally slows down performance since extra work must be done when the code is being executed. Python is so seldom employed in situations where rapid acceleration is needed.

- Python has a very high memory usage rate. This is so that it can accommodate different data kinds. It makes heavy use of memory. Python is not a suitable option for memory-intensive activities if the user wishes to optimize memory use.

- Python is a great server-side programming language because it performs well on desktop and server platforms, which is important for mobile development. However, it is not suitable for mobile development. Python is a vulnerable language when used for mobile development. Due to the fact that it uses a lot of memory and has a slow processing speed, Python does not have many native mobile apps. Python comes with a built-in program called Carbuncle.

- Access to databases is made simple by Python

programming. However, various problems occur when it communicates with the database. The database access layer of the Python programming language is basic and immature in comparison to relatively well-known technologies like JDBC and ODBC. Large businesses often do not favor the use of Python when they require easy interaction with complicated historical data.

- Runtime errors: Python users identified a number of problems with the language's structure. The data type of a variable may change at any moment since Python is a dynamically typed language. As a result, it requires additional testing, and runtime defects in the language are also present.

- Python is a clear and user-friendly programming language, which is also one of its drawbacks. Python users have trouble learning other programming languages because of their comfort with its simple syntax and large collection of features. Due to their intricacy, some users believe the Java programs are unneeded. Because of this, Python is very fragile, and users begin to take things for granted.